This Is a Let's-Read-and-Find-Out Science Book®

Rockets and Satellites

Second
Revised Edition

by Franklyn M. Branley

illustrated by Giulio Maestro

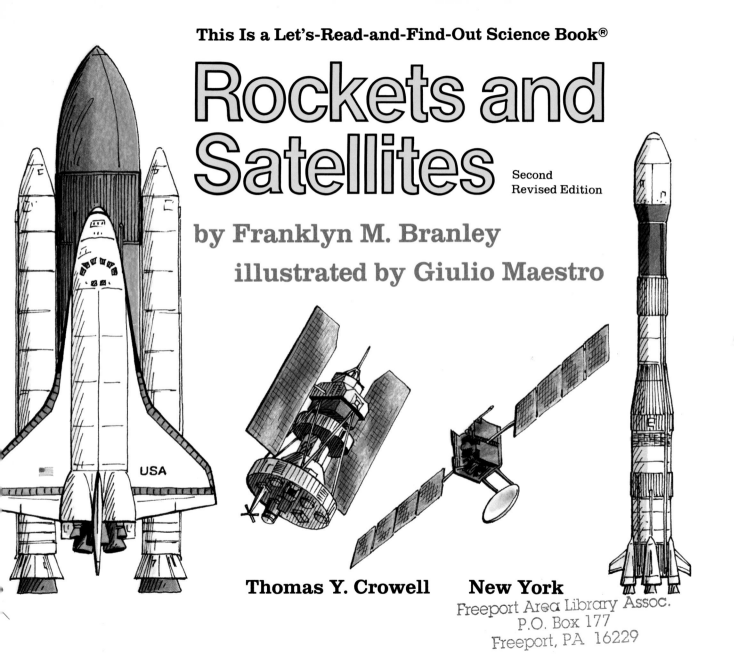

Thomas Y. Crowell   **New York**

Other Recent Let's-Read-and-Find-Out Science Books® You Will Enjoy

Shooting Stars • A Drop of Blood • My Five Senses • What Happened to the Dinosaurs? • Switch On, Switch Off • Ducks Don't Get Wet • Feel the Wind • The Skeleton Inside You • Digging Up Dinosaurs • Tornado Alert • The Sun: Our Nearest Star • The Beginning of the Earth • Eclipse • Dinosaur Bones • Glaciers • Snakes Are Hunters • Danger—Icebergs! • Comets • Evolution • Rockets and Satellites • The Planets in Our Solar System • The Moon Seems to Change • Ant Cities • Get Ready for Robots! • Gravity Is a Mystery • Snow Is Falling • Journey into a Black Hole • What Makes Day and Night • Air Is All Around You • Turtle Talk • What the Moon Is Like • Hurricane Watch • Sunshine Makes the Seasons • My Visit to the Dinosaurs • The BASIC Book • Bits and Bytes • Germs Make Me Sick! • Flash, Crash, Rumble, and Roll • Volcanoes • Dinosaurs Are Different • What Happens to a Hamburger • Meet the Computer • How to Talk to Your Computer • Rock Collecting • Is There Life in Outer Space? • All Kinds of Feet • Flying Giants of Long Ago • Rain and Hail • Why I Cough, Sneeze, Shiver, Hiccup & Yawn • You Can't Make a Move Without Your Muscles • The Sky Is Full of Stars • No Measles, No Mumps for Me

The *Let's-Read-and-Find-Out Science Book* series was originated by Dr. Franklyn M. Branley, Astronomer Emeritus and former Chairman of the American Museum-Hayden Planetarium, and was formerly co-edited by him and Dr. Roma Gans, Professor Emeritus of Childhood Education, Teachers College, Columbia University. For a complete catalog of Let's-Read-and-Find-Out Science Books, write to Thomas Y. Crowell Junior Books, Harper & Row, Publishers, Inc., 10 East 53rd Street, New York, NY 10022.

Rockets and Satellites
Text copyright © 1961, 1970, 1987 by Franklyn M. Branley
Illustrations copyright © 1987 by Giulio Maestro
All rights reserved. No part of this book may be used or reproduced in any manner whatsoever without written permission except in the case of brief quotations embodied in critical articles and reviews. Printed in the United States of America. For information address Thomas Y. Crowell Junior Books, 10 East 53rd Street, New York, N.Y. 10022.
Second Revised Edition
10 9 8 7 6 5 4 3 2

Library of Congress Cataloging-in-Publication Data
Branley, Franklyn Mansfield, 1915–
Rockets and satellites.

(Let's-read-and-find-out science book)
Summary: Simple text with illustrations explains rockets and satellites and describes their capabilities and functions.
1. Rockets (Aeronautics)—Juvenile literature.
2. Artificial satellites—Juvenile literature.
[1. Rockets (Aeronautics) 2. Artificial satellites]
I. Maestro, Giulio, ill. II. Title. III. Series.
TL782.5.B73 1987   629.4   86-47748
ISBN 0-690-04591-3
ISBN 0-690-04593-X (lib. bdg.)

(Let's-read-and-find-out book)
"A Harper trophy book."
ISBN 0-06-445061-9 (pbk.)   86-27047

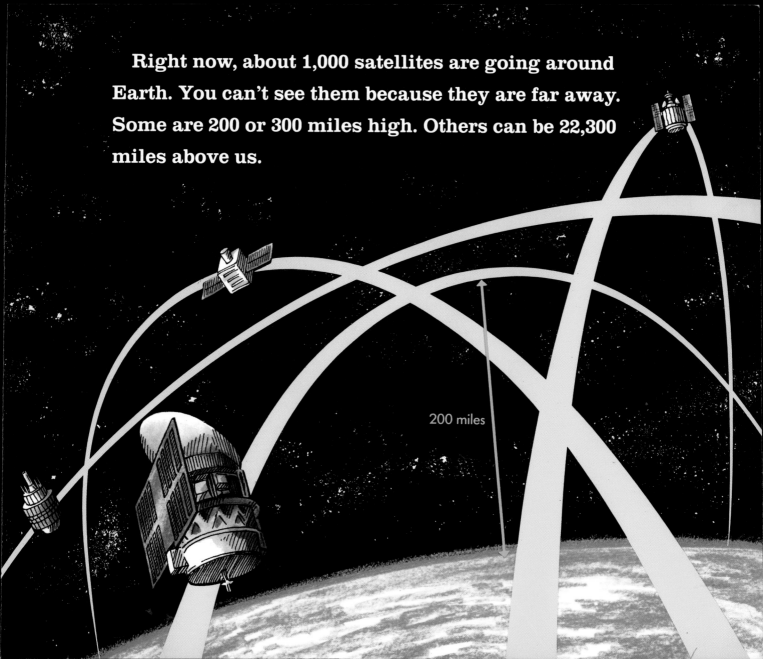

Right now, about 1,000 satellites are going around Earth. You can't see them because they are far away. Some are 200 or 300 miles high. Others can be 22,300 miles above us.

200 miles

All of them are in orbit around Earth. Satellites go very fast. Those close to Earth take only 90 minutes to go around the planet. Satellites farther out take 24 hours to go once around.

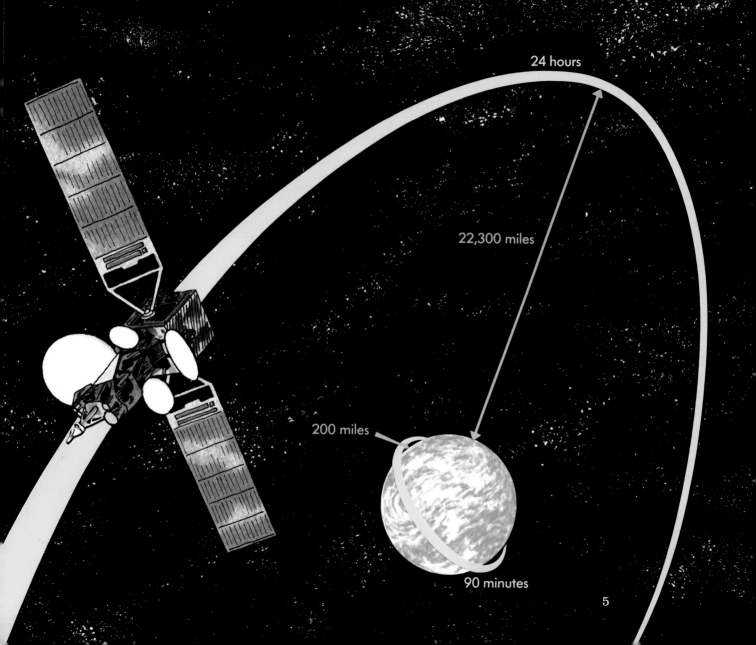

24 hours

22,300 miles

200 miles

90 minutes

5

Satellites stay in orbit because they move very fast. Suppose you were at the top of a high tower and you threw a ball straight out. The ball would travel a hundred feet or so and fall back to Earth. Earth's gravity would pull it down. If you threw the ball faster, it would travel farther. But it would also fall to Earth.

Suppose you could throw a ball as fast as a rocket goes. It would travel much farther. Earth's gravity would pull on it. But the curve of its fall would be the same as the curve of Earth's surface. The ball would not fall to Earth. It would be in orbit.

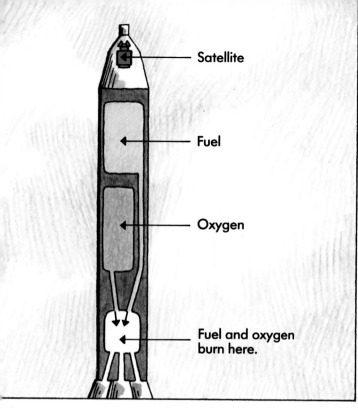

Satellite

Fuel

Oxygen

Fuel and oxygen
burn here.

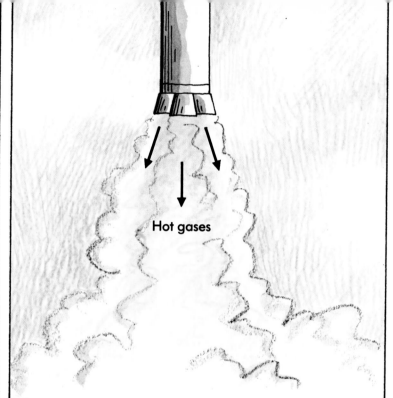

Hot gases

That's what happens with satellites. A rocket puts a satellite into orbit, but it doesn't go into orbit itself. A rocket pushes a satellite to high speeds.

Rockets carry a lot of fuel that burns very fast. When the fuel burns, gases form.

The gases are pushed out of the rocket, and the rocket moves ahead. It's somewhat like a balloon. Blow up a balloon with air, and then let it go. The air is a gas. As the air leaves, the balloon scoots away.

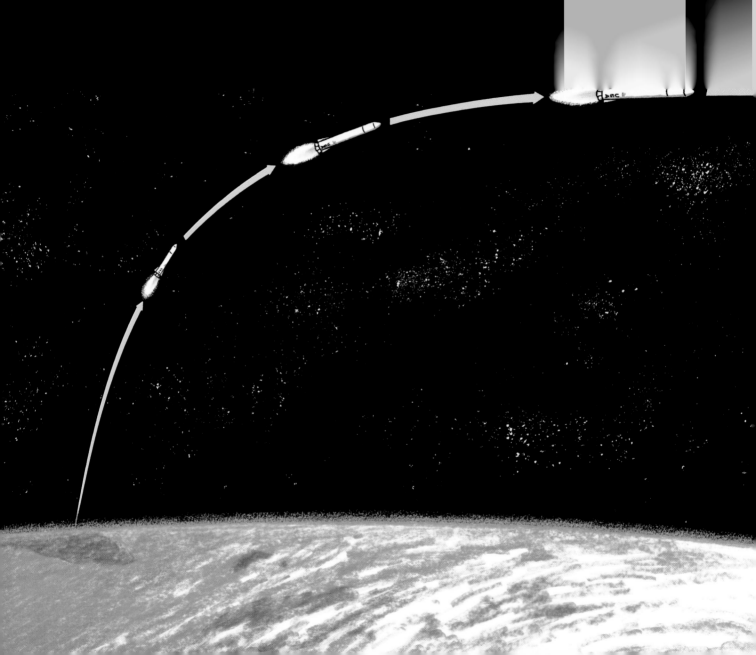

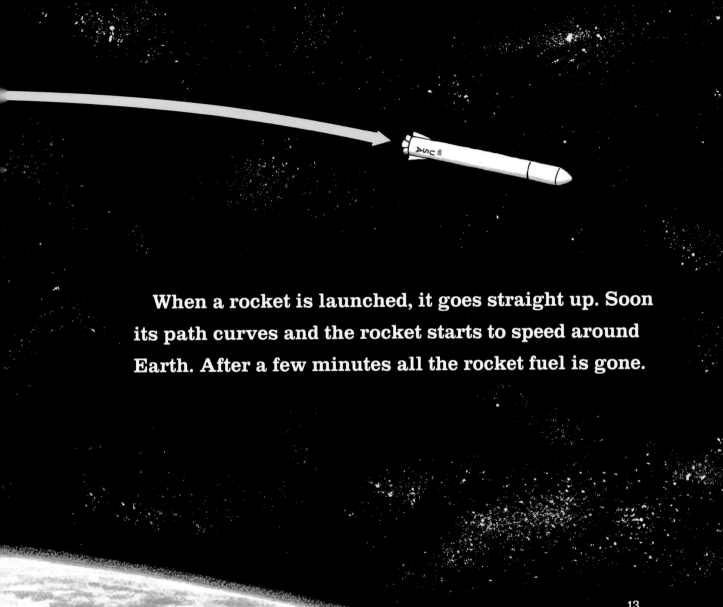

When a rocket is launched, it goes straight up. Soon its path curves and the rocket starts to speed around Earth. After a few minutes all the rocket fuel is gone.

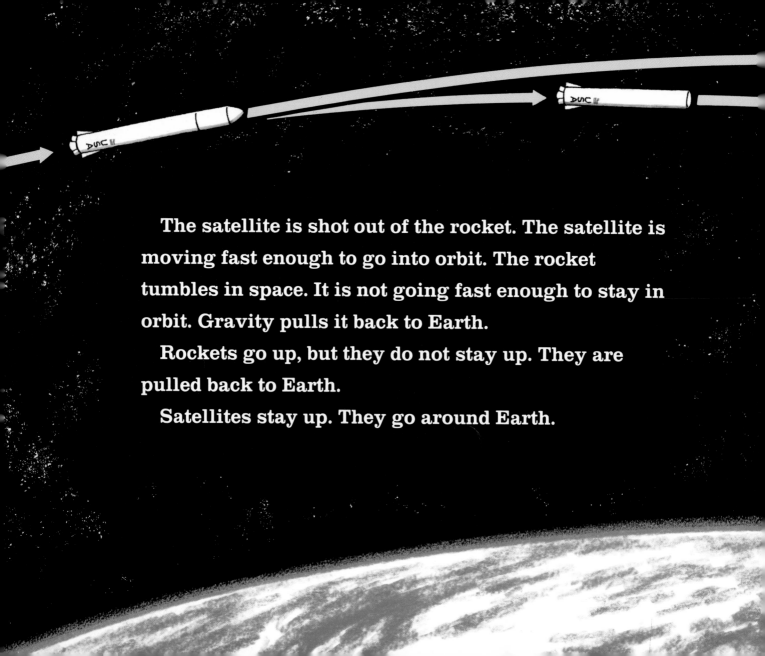

The satellite is shot out of the rocket. The satellite is moving fast enough to go into orbit. The rocket tumbles in space. It is not going fast enough to stay in orbit. Gravity pulls it back to Earth.

Rockets go up, but they do not stay up. They are pulled back to Earth.

Satellites stay up. They go around Earth.

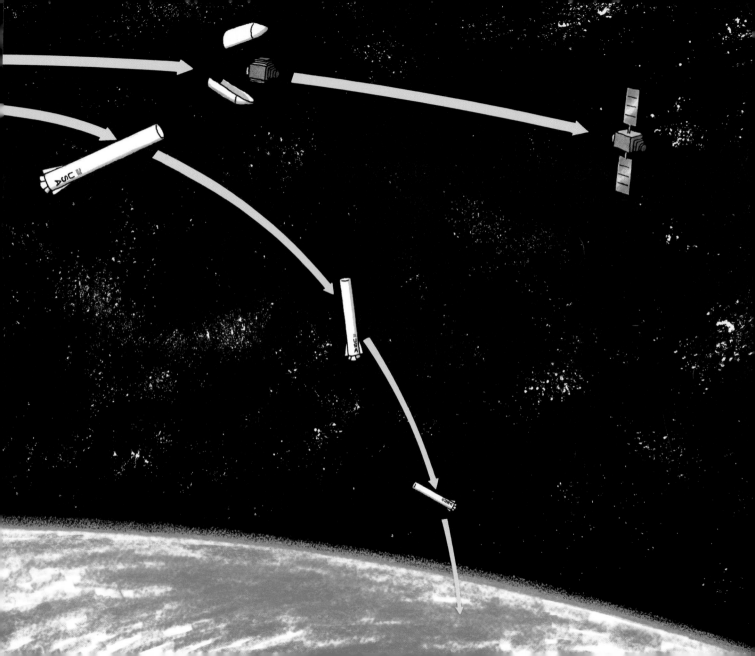

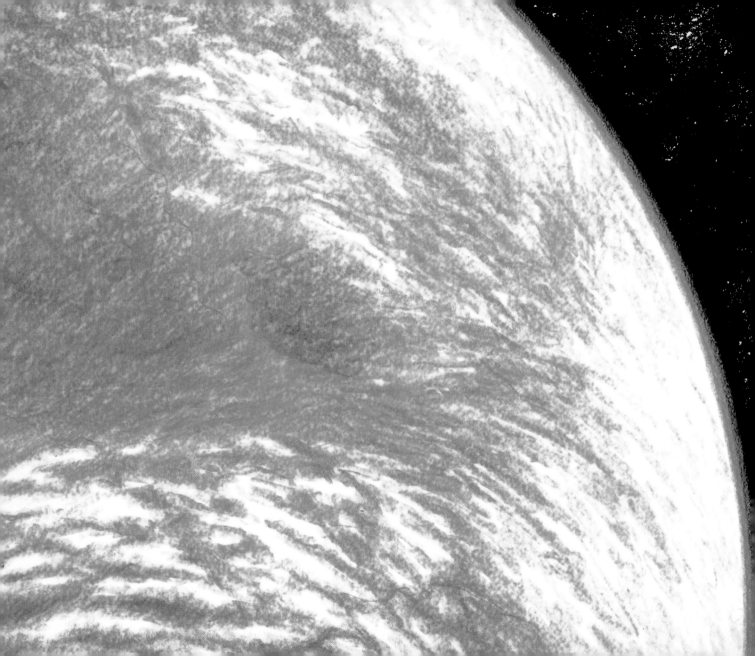

Some satellites take pictures. Weather satellites take pictures of clouds and storms. Other satellites take pictures of fields, lakes, and forests. Satellites send television programs and telephone messages from one part of the world to another.

Some satellites carry telescopes for looking at the stars. The largest is the Hubble telescope. These satellites are above most of Earth's atmosphere, and so they can see stars clearly. In the next few years satellite telescopes may discover planets going around some stars.

Satellites may carry space factories. The factories may make medicines and other products that cannot be made here on Earth.

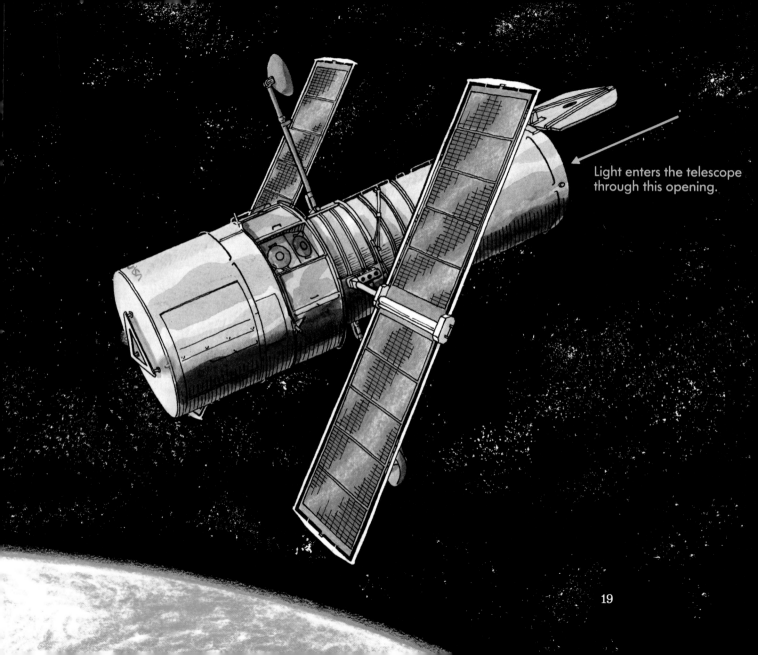

Light enters the telescope through this opening.

Every kind of satellite must be launched by a rocket or by a space shuttle.

Rockets are one-way space taxis. They carry satellites only once; and then they fall back to Earth. Some rockets, or pieces of them, stay in orbit for quite a while before they fall to Earth. They are pieces of space junk, as small as a dime or as big as a car. Several thousand of them are in space right now.

Shuttles also launch satellites. They are space buses, for they carry three or four satellites. And they can go up again and again.

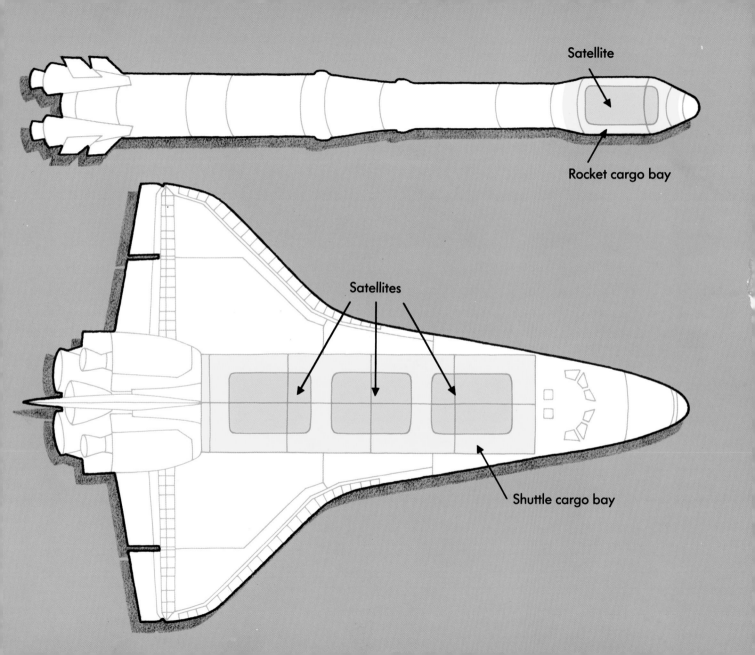

Satellite

Rocket cargo bay

Satellites

Shuttle cargo bay

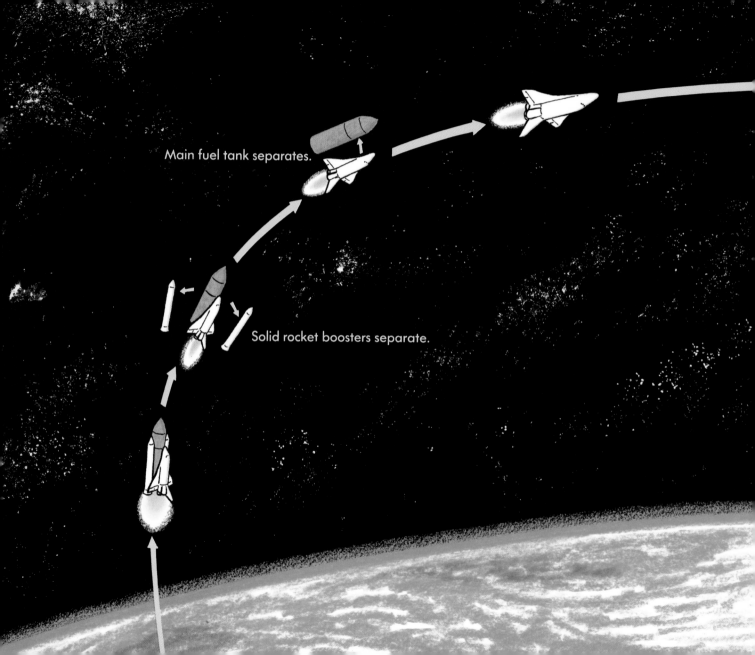

Main fuel tank separates.

Solid rocket boosters separate.

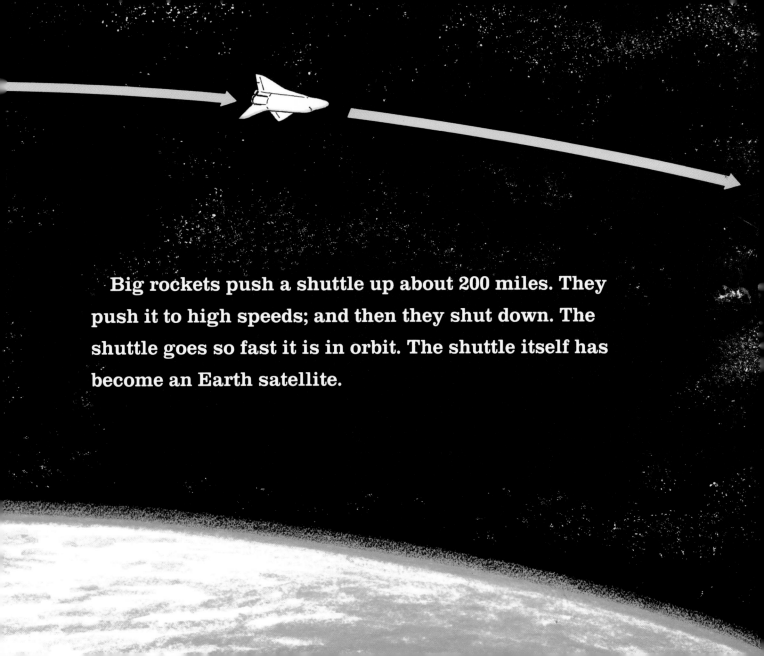

Big rockets push a shuttle up about 200 miles. They push it to high speeds; and then they shut down. The shuttle goes so fast it is in orbit. The shuttle itself has become an Earth satellite.

When the shuttle is in orbit, springs push the satellites out of the cargo bay. Or, the remote manipulator arm of the shuttle lifts the satellites out of the bay.

When the satellites are put overboard, they are in orbit. Television satellites have small rockets fastened to them.

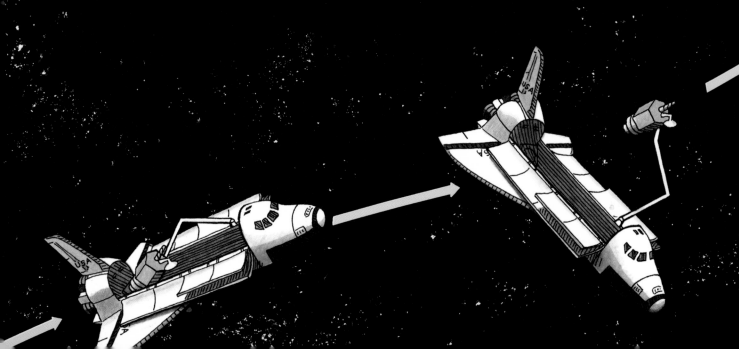

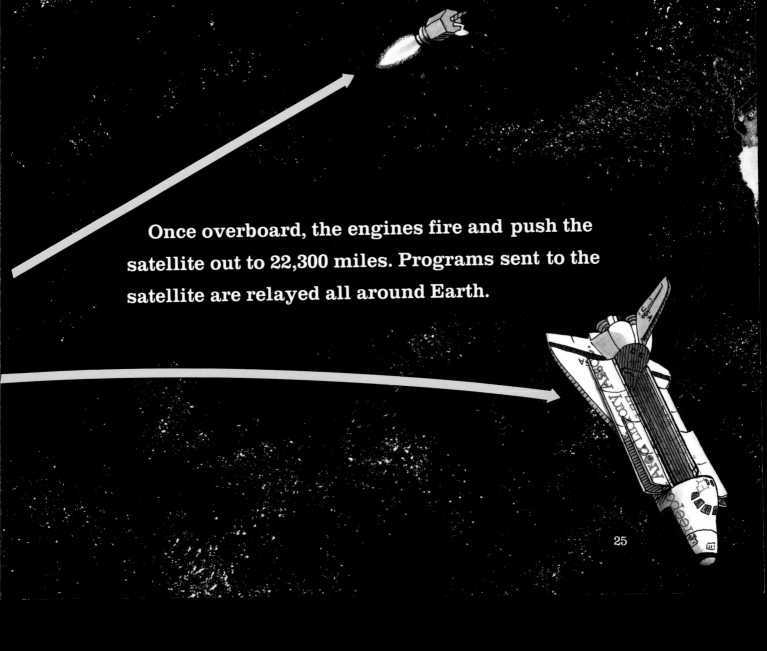

Once overboard, the engines fire and push the satellite out to 22,300 miles. Programs sent to the satellite are relayed all around Earth.

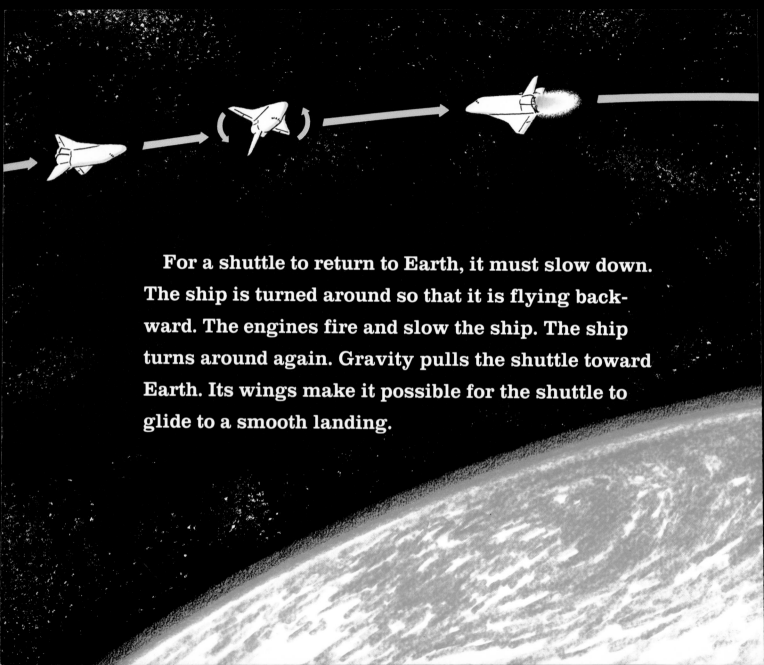

For a shuttle to return to Earth, it must slow down. The ship is turned around so that it is flying backward. The engines fire and slow the ship. The ship turns around again. Gravity pulls the shuttle toward Earth. Its wings make it possible for the shuttle to glide to a smooth landing.

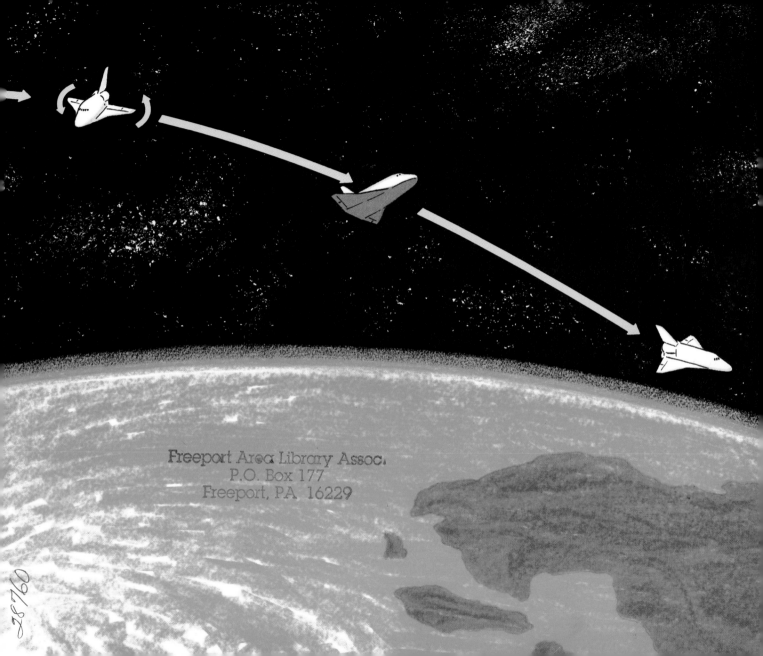

Before the year 2000, shuttles may carry parts for a space station. Astronauts will build the station in space. It will be another Earth satellite—a station in orbit.

Men and women will live and work there. Each team of six to eight people will spend several months aboard the station. Then another team will take over.

Satellites don't last forever. Parts wear out. Batteries aboard some of them run down.

Shuttle astronauts have captured satellites and brought them back to the shuttle. They fixed them and put them back into orbit.

When the space station is built, one of the jobs of the teams aboard it will be to keep satellites working.

Today 1,000 satellites are in orbit around Earth. Each year there are more of them. There will be more rockets and shuttles to launch them. Satellites are changing the way we live, and they will change it a lot more in the next few years.